GENIUS ENGINEERING INVENTIONS

FROM THE PLOW TO 3D PRINTING

Thanks to the creative team:
Senior Editor: Alice Peebles
Fact Checking: Tom Jackson
Design: www.collaborate.agency

Hungry Tomato®
A division of Lerner Publishing Group, Inc.
241 First Avenue North
Minneapolis, MN 55401 USA

For reading levels and more information, look up
this title at www.lernerbooks.com.

Main body text set in Josefin Slab SemiBold 10.5/12.
Typeface provided by Font Squirrel.

Library of Congress Cataloging-in-Publication Data

Names: Turner, Matt, 1964- author. | Conner, Sarah, author.
Title: Genius engineering inventions : from the plow to 3D
        printing / Matt Turner, Sarah Conner.
Description: Minneapolis : Hungry Tomato, [2018] | Series:
        Incredible inventions | Includes index.
Identifiers: LCCN 2016059590 (print) | LCCN 2017003567
        (ebook) | ISBN 9781512432114 (lb : alk. paper) | ISBN
        9781512450095 (eb pdf)
Subjects: LCSH: Inventions—Juvenile literature.
Classification: LCC T15 .T82 2018 (print) | LCC T15 (ebook) | DDC
        600—dc23

LC record available at https://lccn.loc.gov/2016059590

Manufactured in the United States of America
1-41766-23527-3/3/2017

GENIUS ENGINEERING INVENTIONS

FROM THE PLOW TO 3D PRINTING

by Matt Turner
Illustrated by Sarah Connor

HUNGRY TOMATO®

Minneapolis

Nylon was invented in the 1930s to make stockings—but was also used for parachutes and other war supplies.

CONTENTS

MAKING PROGRESS

The society we live in is in a constant state of reinvention. Every day, new products and ideas come to market. Some are excellent, like the electric motor or the heart pacemaker, while others are not so good—for example, Thomas Edison's giant gelatin-mold houses. But these ideas all add to a history of innovation that dates back thousands of years to when our ancestors first came up with the plow, the wheel, the clock, and the countless other everyday items we take for granted. And they all shape society. Electricity gives us instant communication, convenient kitchen gadgets, and clean transport. Medical advances have added years to the average life span.

Medieval moldboard plow, ninth century

Antiseptic surgery, 1860s

We can't always know who had the brainwaves behind these inventions first. Often, it's just the gradual march of forward progress. But every once in a while comes a leap of imagination or a chance discovery that leads to a new idea. The popsicle, for instance, was invented by accident when a soda drink was left out on a freezing-cold doorstep!

Bessemer converter, 1856

Genius Engineering Inventions takes us through the fascinating history of inventions that have created our world, from earliest times, through the turmoil of the industrial revolution, to the present day. Along the way, we'll look at what we eat (and how we grow it), the rise of steam power and electricity, keeping track of time, inventions around the home, medical milestones, smart manufacturing, and the creation of wonder materials like Velcro and Kevlar. And hopefully you'll learn that anyone—including you—can change the way we live today through a clever idea.

Water frame, 1767

Velcro, 1955

AGRICULTURE

Farming these days involves high technology, big tractors, and complex soil science—but it still relies on the ancient inventions, such as the plow and windmill, which our ancestors first used to tame wild land and make it productive.

SIMPLE PLOW

Once we had domesticated cattle, perhaps 8,000 years ago, the ard followed. This simple plow made from wood—and later metal—scratched single furrows in the soil.

HEAVY PLOW

On this ninth-century heavy plow, a coulter blade makes the first cut in the soil. Behind that are the share and moldboard, which turn the soil over.

SHADUF

Ancient Egyptians used the shaduf to draw water. On the short end, a weight of clay or stone balanced the bucket end, making it easy for one person to lift.

Hey chum, jump on and I'll give you a lift.

What about us?

WHEELBARROW

Who invented the wheelbarrow? No one's quite sure. Possibly it was the ancient Greeks. But certainly the early Chinese were using it by around 200 CE. It was also the Chinese who first domesticated pigs and chickens.

LIGHTWEIGHT PLOW

This plow from 1730, designed in Rotherham, England by Joseph Foljambe, was simple to build, and its iron-clad moldboard made a clean cut.

TRACTOR

You can hitch a modern-day, multi-bladed plow (or any other farming tool) to the back of a tractor. The tool uses power supplied by the tractor's engine..

WINDMILLS

The first windmills were probably invented in eighth-century Persia for grinding grain or drawing water. They worked sideways, turning horizontally inside walls that funnelled the wind through the vanes.

ARCHIMEDES SCREW

The Archimedes screw lifts water by turning a spiral. It's named after the Greek genius Archimedes (287-212 BCE), but it may have been invented centuries before he was born.

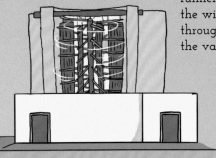

WATERWHEELS

Some 2,000 years ago at Barbegal in France, the Romans built a staircase of 16 connected waterwheels. (The picture shows just the bottom wheel.) They used the mill to grind grain into flour.

FOOD TECHNOLOGY

Your kitchen pantry probably contains cans and jars of preserved food. And you'll have devices to keep food cool (a fridge) or hot (a thermal flask). But centuries ago, there were no such conveniences—not even ovens. So who invented them all?

FIRST CAN

In 1810, Frenchman Nicolas Appert came up with the first can. He sealed food in a glass jar capped with cork and wax and boiled it. It would then stay fresh. To prove the method, he once preserved a whole sheep!

> Duh, no label—hope it's peas, not dog food.

RING PULL

The ring pull on a drink can was invented in the USA in 1959 by Ermal "Ernie" Fraze. Within two decades, his company was earning half a billion dollars a year from his clever little tab.

TIN CAN

These are the world's first tin cans, made in London in 1813 by the firm of Donkin, Hall & Gamble. Trouble was, the can opener wasn't invented until 1855! That's why these men are opening the cans with a hammer and chisel.

THERMOS

Around 1892, Scottish chemist James Dewar invented the vacuum flask for keeping liquids cold (or hot). Sadly, he didn't patent the idea, but the German company Thermos did ... and the rest is history.

Cool. But what is it again?

What do you think?

FIRST FRIDGE

The first fridge was this ice machine, invented in America by Oliver Evans and built by Jacob Perkins in 1834. It used a terrifically complicated pumping system to remove heat and cool the water.

FRANKLIN STOVE

In 1741, brilliant American Ben Franklin invented a fireplace with openings that let out more heat without lots of smoke. Modestly, he called it the Franklin stove.

Now will you invent something to scrape it off the floor?

PROPERTY OF Coca-Cola BOTTLING CO

COCA-COLA

In 1886 in Atlanta, Georgia, American chemist John "Doc" Pemberton began selling a fizzy drink as a *brain tonic*, which he described as "pure joy." Its name? Coca-Cola.

CHEWING GUM

You could cook on a Franklin stove too. Here, John B. Curtis is heating a pot of sticky resin from spruce trees in 1848 to make America's first chewing gum.

IRON AND STEAM

With the invention of the steam engine three centuries ago and, with it, the ability to make plenty of good iron and steel, the Western world entered the Industrial Revolution. Steam, on its own or in partnership with electricity, would power the new factories, steamboats, and railway locomotives.

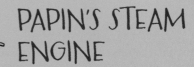

> You're selling us down the river!

> Oh, just go with the flow.

PAPIN'S STEAM ENGINE

French-born physicist Denis Papin, helped by Gottfried Leibniz, invented one of the first steam engines in 1707 and planned to fit it to a steamboat. But the boatmen on the river Weser in Germany, afraid of the new technology, stopped him carrying out his plan.

PURE IRON

To build the early steam engines they needed good, pure iron—lots of it. In 1709, Englishman Abraham Darby I worked out how to purify iron by heating it with coke (coal that has been cooked). Newcomen's pumping engine used iron from Darby's furnaces.

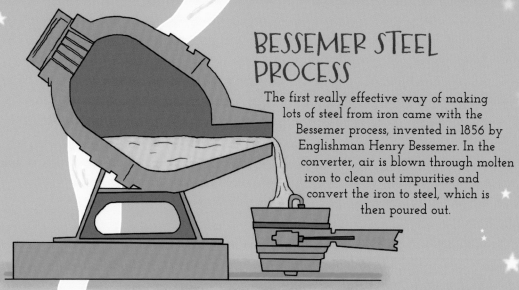

BESSEMER STEEL PROCESS

The first really effective way of making lots of steel from iron came with the Bessemer process, invented in 1856 by Englishman Henry Bessemer. In the converter, air is blown through molten iron to clean out impurities and convert the iron to steel, which is then poured out.

HIGH-PRESSURE STEAM ENGINE

The first steam engines used low pressure and were not very powerful. That changed with the high-pressure steam engine, invented by Englishman Richard Trevithick in the 1790s. It would drive industrial machines, steamboats, and the world's first railway locomotive.

Rocker beam

Hot water back to boiler

Steam from boiler

Hot water from condensed steam recycles back to boiler

Piston in cyclinder

Cooling water

PUMPING ENGINE

In England in 1712, Thomas Newcomen used Papin's ideas in his steam-powered engine for pumping water from coal mines. In the 1770s, Matthew Boulton and James Watt added a condensing cylinder to Newcomen's design. Their pumping engine (*right*) was much more efficient.

Hot water

Vacuum pump   Condenser

THE TEXTILE REVOLUTION

The steam engines of the Industrial Revolution and water power meant new machines for making goods, such as woven cloth, in greater quantities than ever before. Society changed dramatically as country folk crowded into towns to work in the new factories.

SPINNING WHEEL

In earlier times, making yarn from wool was slow work. The spinning wheel, invented around 1000 CE in India, sped things up, but spinners still found it hard to supply weavers with enough yarn.

Baaaa!

AMERICAN WEAVING

Industrial weaving came to the US thanks to Francis Lowell, who had secretly copied British loom designs during a visit from 1810-1812. He built textile mills in Massachusetts and fitted them with his new, improved looms.

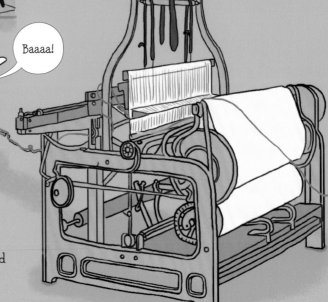

JETHRO TULL

The revolution in mechanized work reached agriculture too. The English seed drill, invented in 1701 by Jethro Tull, planted seeds in holes at the right growing depth. Before, seeds had just been thrown across the soil.

SPINNING JENNY

In 1764, Englishman James Hargreaves invented the spinning jenny, a machine that could spin several spools of yarn at once. One machine did the job of eight, ten, or even one hundred spinners.

The machine's name, *jenny*, probably came from the word engine.

Why do they keep calling me Jenny? I'm Maggie.

WATER FRAME

Richard Arkwright's water frame (1767) was a yarn spinner powered by water flow. In his Nottingham factory, belts, pulleys, and shafts connected a water wheel to each floor, driving the frames.

ELECTRICITY

Electricity has a long history. Early persons knew about electric fish, lightning, and static electricity (the crackly tingle you get sometimes by stroking a cat's fur, for instance). But storing electricity and using it as a power source dates from 350 years ago.

LEYDEN JAR

This is a Leyden jar. It's a very crude battery or capacitor, capable of storing electricity. It was invented around 1745 by Ewald von Kleist in Germany and Pieter van Musschenbroek in Leiden, Holland.

Cork lid

Glass jar

Tin foil inner lining

Tin foil outer lining

Water

Electrode (metal rod and chain)

TESLA COIL

Serbian Nikola Tesla (1856-1943) pioneered radio, neon lights, alternating current, X-rays, Wi-Fi, and even a "death ray" (which, luckily, he didn't build). His Tesla coil is a kind of transformer.

You can wire me to the mains!

CATCHING LIGHTNING

It's said that in 1752 Ben Franklin—or his son—flew a kite to "catch" lightning and store it in a Leyden jar, but he probably never did. He did realize, though, that lightning equals electricity. And he invented the lightning rod, and the word *battery*.

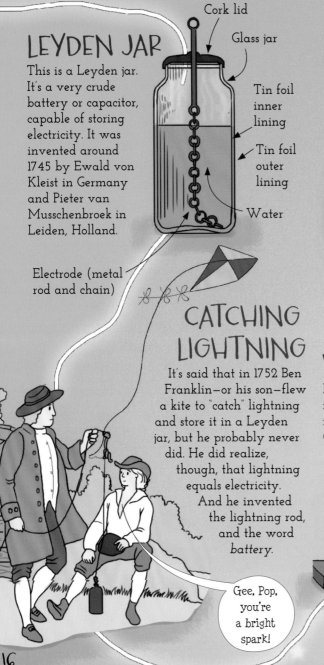

Gee, Pop, you're a bright spark!

VOLTAIC PILE

Italian scientist Alessandro Volta invented his voltaic pile, a battery, in the 1790s. His countryman Luigi Galvani had earlier found that if you sent electricity through a dead frog's legs, they twitched—showing that nerve signals are electric messages.

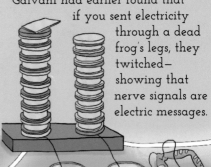

ELECTRIFYING INVENTOR

Frenchman Gustave Trouvé (1839-1902) designed this glowing jewellery. The list of his electrified inventions includes a canoe, an outboard motor, a dentist's drill (ouch), a metal detector, an airship, a razor, a sewing machine, a microphone, a telegraph, a rifle, and more.

My bling may be "light," but it feels sooo heavy!

LIGHTNING ROD

The 19th century saw a craze for all things electrical. This man has a Franklin rod attached to his umbrella to ward against lightning strikes.

HYDROELECTRIC POWER

The first house to run on hydroelectric power (from water flow) was Cragside in England. Its dynamos provided lighting and powered the nearby farm buildings.

ELECTRIC MOTOR

In 1871, Zénobe Gramme, a Belgian, invented an electric generator or dynamo. It wasn't very good—but he later found (by accident) that his machine, if connected to an electric source, would spin by itself. He had invented the modern electric motor.

Oops! But then again, hurrah!

FARADAY DISK

English scientist Michael Faraday made the crucial connection between electricity and magnetism. He invented an early electric generator, the Faraday disk, in 1831. It works by spinning a metal flywheel in a magnetic field.

MEASURING TIME

We've come up with all sorts of inventions to measure the passage of time. The ancients saw the sun rise and set each day and very sensibly used it to measure the hours. Of course, sundials don't work in the dark, so the clockwork mechanism was the next leap forward.

3D SUNDIAL

This 3D sundial, invented in 250 BCE by Greek astronomer Aristarchus, is called a scaphe. The post casts a shadow inside the hemisphere, showing the time. Aristarchus, by the way, used it to calculate Earth's size and distance from the Moon.

WATER CLOCK

The ancient Egyptians relied on the water clock, or clepsydra: water dripped from one container into another to measure the hours. (They used it to time people's speeches during debates. No more drip: zip your lip!)

Oh look, it's time for tea!

Humph! Tea break is over.

SUPER TIMER

A water clock designed in the third century BCE by Ctesibius of Alexandria is said to have been the most accurate timekeeper of the next 1,800 years.

Mechanical bird (makes chirping sound)

ELEPHANT CLOCK

In 1206, the Muslim engineer Al Jazari invented this water-powered elephant clock, which made a sound every half-hour. It borrowed technologies from many ancient cultures, including Indian, Persian, Chinese, and Greek.

Hidden water mechanism

Chinese dragon (tips when a ball is dropped into its mouth)

PENDULUM CLOCK

Driver (hits a drum every half-hour)

Time for a nap, I reckon!

This pendulum clock, designed in the 1650s by Dutch astronomer Christiaan Huygens, was more accurate than any clock made over the next two and a half centuries. (A pendulum is a weight on an arm, which swings regularly to keep time.)

Elephant statue

TICK

TOCK TICK TOCK TICK TOCK TICK TOCK TICK TOCK TICK

WHAT'S THE WEATHER?

Vacuum

Mercury

Glass column

The level of mercury rises or falls with changing air pressure

One way of forecasting the weather is to measure atmospheric pressure using a barometer. This early barometer of 1643 was the invention of Italian Evangelista Torricelli. It reads the changing height of a column of mercury, a liquid metal.

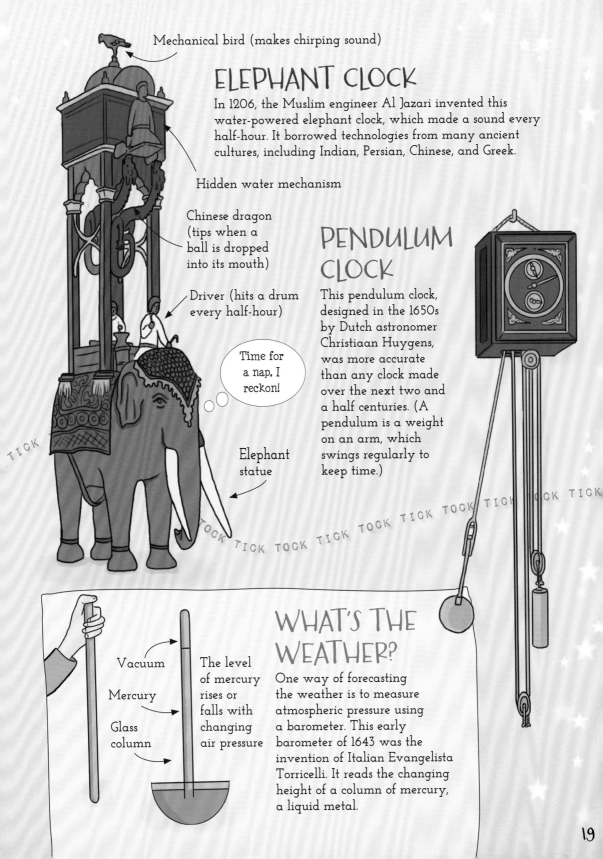

AT HOME

Take a look around your home and school. Some of the basic materials—glass, concrete, brick—date back to ancient civilizations, and it's hard to say exactly who invented them. But all those nifty devices, such as locks, doorbells, elevators, and toilets came from someone's brainwave.

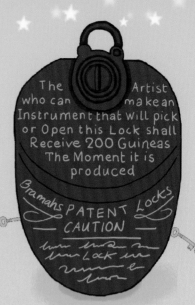

The ___ Artist who can ___ make an Instrument that will pick or Open this Lock shall Receive 200 Guineas The Moment it is produced

Bramahs PATENT Locks — CAUTION —

PIN LOCK

Over 2,000 years ago, the Mesopotamians used key-operated door locks, made from timber. This is an ancient Egyptian pin lock.

CHALLENGE LOCK

High-security locks date back to 1784, when British engineer Joseph Bramah designed his Challenge lock. He promised a big cash prize to the first person to pick it (unlock it without a key). It remained unpicked for sixty-seven years! By then, of course, old Joe had died.

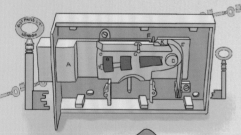

CHUBB LOCK

English locksmith Jeremiah Chubb invented this *detector lock* in 1818. If you used the wrong key in it, the lock jammed and could only be opened with a special extra key (*right*).

ELECTRIC DOORBELL

In 1831, American scientist Joseph Henry invented a doorbell that rang inside a building via an electric wire. Yep. We have him to thank for all those kids who ring the bell and run away. The electric relay in Joe's bell was later used by Samuel Morse in the Morse code tapper.

I could get tired of this.

Gotta keep it moving...

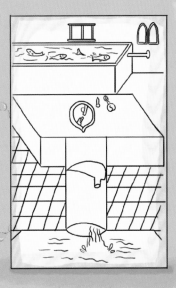

TOILETS

If there's one home invention we use every day, it's the toilet, also called a loo. It's an old one too. The Romans had toilets with drains to flush away the poo, and they wiped their bums with a sponge on a stick.

FLUSHING TOILETS

In 1596, English writer Sir John Harington drew this design for the Ajax, the world's first true flushing toilet. In his day it was called "the jakes." He probably didn't really keep fish in the water tank, though!

BUILT TO LAST

Locksmith Joseph Bramah also designed flushing toilets. Some of the ones he built in his London workshop are still working.

SAFETY ELEVATOR

Early elevators were dangerous: if their lifting cable broke, they could barrel to the ground, killing the passengers. So, American Elisha Otis invented a safety elevator with an emergency brake and demonstrated it at New York's World Fair in 1854. The cable was cut, and Elisha fell just a few inches in his elevator before the brake stopped it. Success!

Now all we need is elevator music.

MATERIALS

Perhaps you've never heard of materials science, but it's big business. Inventors are constantly at work improving the stuff things are made of–making it cheaper, better at its job, better for the environment, and more. Welcome to the history and science of stuff!

MACKINTOSH

The Mackintosh raincoat was invented by Scotsman Charles Macintosh in the 1820s. He made the waterproof fabric by sandwiching rubber between two layers of cloth.

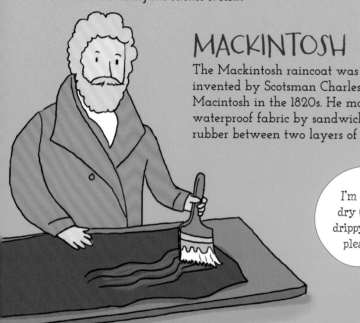

I'm quite dry (so no drippy jokes please!).

VELCRO

Velcro was invented by a dog. Nearly. George de Mestral was walking in Switzerland in 1941 and noticed how the hooked spines of plant burrs stuck to his dog's fur. That gave him the idea for a clingy strip-fastener with one side of "fur" and another of tiny hooks. Velcro was launched in 1955.

Yup, I invented this!

DUPONT INVENTIONS

Workers at the American company DuPont have a knack for inventing new materials. Here's a roundup of some of their most famous.

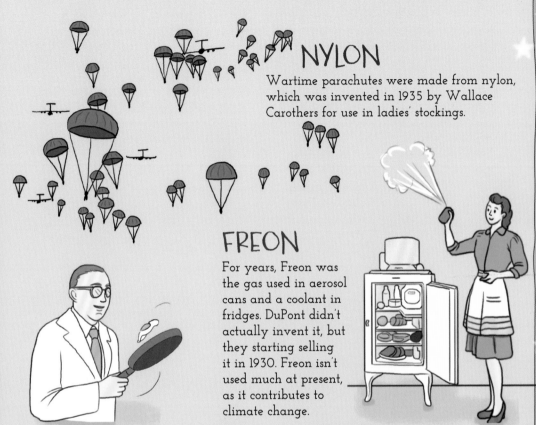

NYLON

Wartime parachutes were made from nylon, which was invented in 1935 by Wallace Carothers for use in ladies' stockings.

FREON

For years, Freon was the gas used in aerosol cans and a coolant in fridges. DuPont didn't actually invent it, but they starting selling it in 1930. Freon isn't used much at present, as it contributes to climate change.

TEFLON

Teflon is the non-stick pan coating that helps your parents flip omelets. Easier to say than polytetrafluoroethylene, it was discovered in 1938 by Roy Plunkett.

GORE-TEX

In 1969, Bob Gore stretched a piece of Teflon to ten times its normal length . . . and found that it turned into a new fabric that was waterproof, yet breathable. We know it as Gore-Tex, and it's used in raincoats and walking boots.

KEVLAR

This police dog wears bullet-proof armour made from Kevlar, a super-tough material invented by chemist Stephanie Kwolek in 1964.

MEDICINE

No book, however big, could be big enough to cover all the fascinating stories of medical discovery and invention. So here are just a few medical milestones–from studying the human body, to pain relief, the prevention of disease, and simple good hygiene.

STUDYING ANATOMY

Dutchman Andries van Wesel (1514-1564), better known as Vesalius, was one of the first scientists to dissect (cut open) dead bodies to see how they worked. He published books full of anatomical drawings.

Can I move now? I've been sitting here for 12 years!

FIRST VACCINE

In 1796, English scientist Edward Jenner injected a boy with cowpox, collected in pus from a milkmaid's blisters. It protected the boy against smallpox, which was a killer disease. Thanks to Jenner's pioneering vaccination work, smallpox is no more.

STETHOSCOPE

French doctor René Laennec invented the stethoscope in 1816, when trying to listen to a patient's heart. He rolled up some paper into a tube, put his ear to one end, and then heard it clearly. Next, he made a wooden tube. Modern day stethoscopes look quite different, but they work the same way.

FALSE TEETH

False teeth were invented centuries ago, possibly in Italy, but some of the most famous were those of US President George Washington (1732-1799). They included teeth from hippos, cows, other people, and maybe also elephants!

LOUIS PASTEUR

The study of germs, disease, and vaccines by French chemist Louis Pasteur has saved countless lives. In 1862, he invented (and gave his name to) pasteurization: heating milk and beer to kill germs. Here, Pasteur looks on as his colleague, Emile Roux, vaccinates a boy against rabies.

Say aaarggh!

HOSPITAL HYGIENE

It's hard to believe, but surgeons used not to wash their hands before performing operations. In 1847, Hungarian doctor Ignaz Semmelweis believed such uncleanliness was somehow spreading germs and killing patients, so he recommended hand-washing. In doing so, he more or less invented hospital hygiene.

The soap's in here somewhere...

ANTISEPTIC SURGERY

From 1867, inspired by Pasteur and Semmelweis, British surgeon Joseph Lister cleaned up operations by spraying his patients with carbolic acid, an antiseptic, or disinfectant. It killed germs and prevented infection setting in.

FACTORIES

It's one thing to invent improved products. It's quite another to invent better ways of *making* them. The mass-production factory has a long history, but these days we know that big factories can cause waste and pollution. So we're working to make them smarter and more efficient.

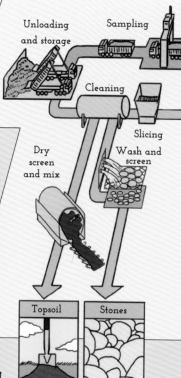

Unloading and storage

Sampling

Cleaning

Slicing

Dry screen and mix

Wash and screen

Topsoil

Stones

I've lost the instruction manual.

MASS PRODUCTION

The ancient Phoenicians were early users of mass production. Their ships were assembled from pre-formed parts, almost like IKEA bookshelves or model kits.

ASSEMBLY LINE

Around 900 years ago, the Venetians were also mass-producing ships. They invented the assembly line, where a product passes from one factory area to another as it's built. American carmaker Henry Ford used the idea in 1913 to assemble his Model T in huge numbers.

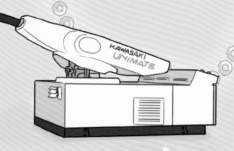

ROBOTS

Modern car factories use computer-programmed robots for jobs that are too dreary, dirty, difficult, or dangerous for human workers. The first industrial robot was this 1950s Unimate arm designed in America by George Devol.

26

Limestone

Sugar beet

Fuel

Weighing

CHP Plant

Electricity →

← Methane

↓ Lime

Steam ↓

CO₂ ↓

Diffusion

Lime kiln

Purification (clarify and filter)

Water (treated) →

River

Evaporation

Low-temperature heat

Filter

Pulp press and drying

Juice storage

Silos

Horticulture

Grade and pack

Resin separation

Ferment and distill

Screen and pack

Animal feed

Lime

Sugar products

Betaine

Bioethanol

Liquid CO₂

Tomatoes

Electricity

Raffinate

Vinasse

Yeast protein

WASTE NOT

This factory in Wissington, England, makes good use of waste. Its main product is sugar (from beets), but by-products include soil, animal feed, tomatoes, electricity, carbon dioxide, fertilizer, and more.

3D PRINTERS

Many modern-day factories include 3D printers. You scan an object (or design it in 3D modeling software) and turn the object file into a language understood by the printer, which then prints the object.

DAFT OR DANGEROUS DUDS

Anybody can come up with new ideas for gadgets and toys, whether they're a famous inventor or someone like you. But that doesn't mean every new idea is a good one—as these examples show!

TALKING DOLLS

Thomas Edison—pioneer of light bulbs, record-players, and movie cameras—had some bad ideas, too. He designed these big dolls for kids in 1890. Each doll contained a gramophone that "sang" nursery rhymes. But they were expensive and made hideous noises that terrified the customers, who sent them back to the shop. Ed later called them "little monsters."

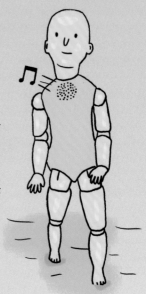

Whaddya mean this is a wobbly idea?

GELATIN-MOLD HOUSES

Back in 1899, poor people needed housing. Ed thought he'd help by casting cheap concrete houses from molds, almost like giant gelatin structures. Only they weren't cheap. They cost forty times more than normal houses! Only one Edison concrete home survived. It is located in Montclair, New Jersey.

HOTTER TROTTER

This 1868 *steam man* was designed by Zadoc Dederick to pull a carriage. It was dressed as a man so as not to frighten horses on the street. It was worse than useless, but it looked fabulous. The top hat cleverly hides the steam exhaust pipe, by the way.

QUAKE-MAKER

Nikola Tesla, electrical genius, also had his off-days. He once invented an earthquake machine, which could (in theory) bring buildings down. He considered it so dangerous, he smashed it with a hammer and never spoke of it again.

Not what I'd call a walk in the park...

BABY ARMOR

In Britain, the threat of an enemy gas attack in the lead-up to World War II led a Mr. Mills to invent this Air Raid Precautions gas-proof baby stroller. There was a window on top so mom could check baby was still breathing.

ACCIDENTAL INVENTIONS

The popsicle was invented by mistake. Here are a few more happy accidents.

Bless you!

PENICILLIN

Scottish biologist Alexander Fleming discovered the disease-killing drug penicillin in 1928 after his nose dripped on a specimen dish in his lab, and it grew moldy.

SLINKY TOY

American Navy engineer Richard James invented the Slinky in 1943. It was going to be a suspension spring for warships, but he found it righted itself when tipped over.

Apparently he's invented a super new glue.

SUPER GLUE

In World War II, American chemist Harry Coover was trying to make gunsights and aircraft canopies out of cyano-acrylate, a clear resin. No such luck—but it was really sticky! We call it contact adhesive, or super glue.

POTATO CHIPS

In 1853 in New York, a diner sent his French fries back, complaining they were too thick. So the chef, George Crum, got grumpy and sliced them ultra-thin, baked them hard, and coated them with salt, intending to make them inedible. But the diner loved them! George had invented potato chips.

Well THAT backfired on me.

I ♥ pacemakers

Boom-boom

IMPLANTABLE PACEMAKER

A pacemaker is an electronic implant that helps unsteady hearts keep a regular beat. American electrical engineer Wilson Greatbatch invented it by mistake in 1956—he used the wrong component while building a recording device. First used in 1960, his pacemaker has since prolonged countless lives.

INDEX

The Author

British-born Matt Turner graduated from Loughborough College of Art in the 1980s, since then he has worked as a picture researcher, editor, and writer. He has authored books on diverse topics, including natural history, earth sciences, and railways, as well as hundreds of articles for encyclopedias and partworks, covering everything from elephants to abstract art. He and his family currently live near Auckland, Aotearoa/New Zealand, where he volunteers for the local Coastguard unit and dabbles in art and craft.

The Illustrator

Sarah Conner lives in the lovely English countryside, in a cute cottage with her dogs and a cat. She spends her days sketching and doodling the world around her. She has always been inspired by nature and it influences much of her work. Sarah formerly used pens and paint for her illustrations, but in recent years she has transferred her style to the computer as it better suits today's industry. However, she still likes to get her watercolors out from time to time and paint the flowers in her garden!